The

Kitchen & Bath

Color Book

ROCKPORT PUBLISHERS

GLOUCESTER MASSACHUSETTS

Melanie and John Aves

First published in the United States of America by:
Rockport Publishers, Inc.
33 Commercial Street
Gloucester, Massachusetts 01930-5089
Telephone: (978) 282-9590
Facsimile: (978) 283-2742

Distributed to the book trade and art trade in the United States by:
North Light Books, an imprint of
F & W Publications
1507 Dana Avenue
Cincinnati, Ohio 45207
Telephone: (800) 289-0963

Other Distribution by:
Rockport Publishers, Inc.
Gloucester, Massachusetts 01930-5089

ISBN 1-56496-470-1

10 9 8 7 6 5 4 3 2 1

Design: Beth Santos Design
Cover Design: Elastic Design
Cover Images: top: Crossville Porcelain Stone Tiles, Mosaic Series, design by
John Buscarello, ASID, photo by Everette Short;
bottom: design by Michael R. Golden, photo by Tim Lee
Back Cover Images: left: design by Norman Michaeloff, photo by Bill Rothschild;
right: design and photo courtesy of Christopher Peacock Kitchens, Inc.

Printed in Hong Kong.

CONTENTS

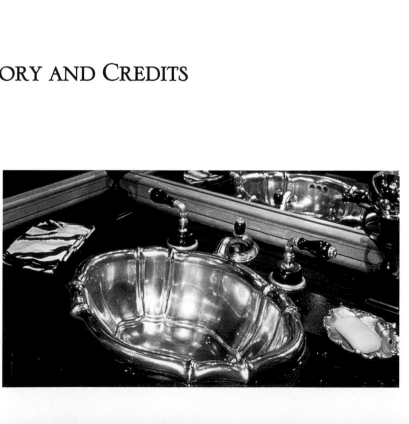

PREFACE

This book is about design decision making. Like all decisions, the quality of the result will depend on the process and the raw materials that are fed into the process. Good design isn't a mystery. It isn't something one must be born with, either.

Good design can be learned by reading and by looking at homes designed by the top professional designers such as those who have graciously contributed illustrations for this book. That intimidating phrase, "good taste," is really another way to describe a good education. People who seem to have intuitive design sense are probably just the product of a lot of good reading, long visits to beautiful spaces and the most important ingredient, the catalyst of curiosity.

We have both been fortunate to have spent our youth with parents who cared enough about home to spend time studying and planning carefully. Then we studied art together in college, and later we found ourselves among many friends and associates who continued adding to our education. We would like to pass our good fortune along to others with the help of the talented editors, designers and publishers at Rockport Publishing, Inc.

The mission of this book and the others we have authored and developed is to make more people aware of the possibilities for comfort and stimulation within their homes, and to build their self confidence. Fear inhibits many people from getting involved in the design process, and fear frequently pushes us toward making the absolutely safe decisions which will not offend anyone…and which will also not bring joy to anyone. Color is one of the most fearsome decisions of all. We hope our readers will unshackle their imaginations and use color to bring comfort, joy and stimulation to the most important people in their lives.

INTRODUCTION TO THE LANGUAGE OF COLOR

The two rooms that add the most value to a home and contribute the most to personal rejuvenation are the kitchen and the bath. They are very important rooms, and can be extremely costly to maintain. The choice of color in these spaces will influence the mood elicited as much as the color applied to any other area of the home; however, design choices can be complicated by the different types of appliances, furnishings, and utilities which may be present. In the kitchen and the bath one must consider the color which appliances, plumbing fixtures, floors, and counter surfaces bring into the space. In other rooms of the home it is usually much easier and less expensive to make changes, because the palette consists of paint, fabric, carpet, and perhaps wallpaper colors.

Not many homeowners are prepared to buy a new refrigerator when they want to change the mood of the kitchen. Perhaps that's a reason many people select neutral color palettes, especially white or beige, for their kitchen and baths. It's a safe decision, likely to stay in style, and the initial purchase of materials is relatively inexpensive. But as applies to most design decisions, the safe choices that satisfy everyone probably don't thrill anybody. Some things never go *out* of style because they are never *in* style. The best personal sanctuaries should inspire on a unique, personal, and timely level.

To properly manage this process, a vocabulary of color is helpful. Although we aim for many subtle reactions when we apply color to a kitchen or bath, the three basic definitions of color that people can readily describe are *hue, brightness*, and *saturation*.

Hue refers to the name of the color. The names revolve around the color wheel, where they can be further categorized as *analogous* (next to each other, like blue and green) or *complementary* (across from each other, like green and red). White and black are not truly colors—they are the absence of color, but are mixed in with other true colors to form a range of neutrals which can be very interesting and subtle.

Another scale of reference is *brightness*, which ranges from white to black. The length of light wavelengths and the reflective quality of a color will have an important effect in determining light levels. This may affect not only mood, but also safety in the functional space of a kitchen or bath.

The third scale is *saturation*, which describes the apparent purity of the color. *Purity* is the absence of white or black.

In our secondary research on the psychological effects of color we have found anecdotal evidence that color has a cause-and-effect relationship on mood. Anger or joy, violence or peacefulness, elation or depression have all been observed as outcomes of various experiments with color in controlled circumstances, such as hospitals, prisons, schools, and businesses. One of our associates was responsible for selecting colors for quarters that would help the first astronauts adjust to their return to earth, an assignment that shows how seriously scientists and designers alike take the effect of color on mood.

◀ A sophisticated showplace with subtle gradations of black appliances, dark gun-metal-color cabinets and gray-streaked countertops, this kitchen is an appropriate stage for the preparation of gourmet meals.

Designer: Rand Elliott, FAIA

▲ Rich color has entered the kitchen with the advent of artfully finished cabinets, colored and rubbed by skilled hands. Note that the
wood finish of the island cabinets is a contrasting natural color, varying
the palette and greatly increasing the appeal of this space. Kitchen
color schemes have evolved beyond monotone monotony.

DESIGN AND PHOTOGRAPHY COURTESY OF CHRISTOPHER PEACOCK KITCHENS, INC.

*Clusters of
color create
a rich palette.*

▲ Details make the difference. The color and pattern in this tile are visually appealing and enhance the appetite!

DESIGNER: BARBARA EBERLEIN

Color comes from many different sources on the ceiling, the walls, and the floor.

◀ ▲ A spectacular architectural plan includes surface colors and texture over, under, and around the fortunate family that gathers in this space. This is a stimulating area that will encourage creative food preparation and bright conversation.

DESIGNER: BARBARA OSTROM

◄ The stainless steel surface is a distinctive color element that also reflects color and light from other surfaces. Some surfaces absorb light and some reflect, another element in a complete plan.

DESIGNER: EURO-CONCEPTS, LTD.

Serenity is created by removing color distractions.

◀ A small bathroom with lacy traditional details that exudes personality. The pink, peach, and red hues cast a healthy reflection.

DESIGNER: ANN HEFFERNAN

Guests can sense the personality of their host through minute details and color choices.

◀ A very dark background with gold fixtures and mirrored ceiling is certain to set a mood of elegance especially appropriate for a guest bathroom. Drama of this intensity is ideal for those who entertain frequently.

DESIGNER (NEAR LEFT): BARBARA EBERLEIN
DESIGNER (FAR LEFT): AUDIO DESIGN ASSOCIATES

Gold and emerald tones are vibrant contrasts that pique the drama of this small space.

◀ A marble-top, floral-decorated chest with the patina of age is a pleasant surprise. This kitchen has the "collector's look," which is difficult to imitate and distinguishes the connoisseur. Detailed carvings in the moldings and surfaces create interesting shadows, one more way to vary the color scheme.

DESIGNER: CATHI MANKOWSKI

Eclectic use of color and material provides sophistication.

◀ Kitchen color plans become wonderfully rich with each material adding a special hue and texture. Copper pots nicely mottled with age, bright ceramic glazes, and a rich tapestry fabric delight the eye in every corner of this invigorating space for creative food preparation.

DESIGNER: BARBARA OSTROM

HIGH EXPECTATIONS FOR THE KITCHEN

The kitchen can be a center for family and friends, an energetic place where the relationships that tie people together on a daily basis can grow. Distinctive color can help set the mood for interaction, and color can enhance all of the other purposes the kitchen serves. There are four predominant roles the kitchen plays; these four functions start with the basics and progress toward a more complex and humanistic set of requirements. It is most logical, therefore, to consider first the neutral palettes, then the more complex and intense analogous colors that are next to each other on the color wheel, ending with contrasting complementary colors that oppose each other on the color wheel.

WORKSPACE Similar to an office, the kitchen must function as an efficient platform for repetitive motion, creative thought, reading, smelling, hearing, and feeling.

COMMUNICATIONS CENTER A home's message center, phone center, and purchasing office are often in the kitchen. This space may be as small as a tray or as large as the administrative manager's office in a small corporation.

SOCIAL AREA Food preparation today is an integral part of our social life, shared by families, friends, and colleagues. People often entertain in the kitchen. Even at formal parties guests will congregate in the kitchen, especially if the host is cooking and serving.

FAMILY NEXUS All of the people in a home interrelate here. So many of the functions, moods, crises, and celebrations happen in this space. The palette, the textures, and the light levels will have a significant effect on how people feel in this room, whether they want to enter, and if they want to stay.

▲ Warm natural wood finish of fine furniture quality softens the black-and-white ceramic backsplash and black counters. The choice of each material is a step in creating the color plan: a dab of white tile, a bold stroke of black granite, a wide wash of natural wood tone.
DESIGNER: DEGUILIO KITCHEN DESIGN, INC.

▶ Another use of creamy yellow, contrasting with black and hard shadow lines. The use of color contrast and lighting creates drama, but this palette requires skilled manipulation.
DESIGNER: GAIL MILLER

COMFORTABLE
NEUTRAL PALETTES

Any color that is very low in intensity can be classified as a neutral. For example, a light salmon color is actually a tint of red, but it is much less intense and therefore it is a good choice for a background color because it will adapt well to many stronger "guest" colors. The neutral palette begins with pure white and ends with black, circling the entire color wheel. Neutrals generally dominate the spectrum in nature, from the brown earth to the white clouds. But, like our environment, there is great variety. And also like our environment, the neutral background colors play host to very intense spots of color.

In the kitchen, neutrals are often used because the permanent color in the surface materials, such as enamel, porcelain, and vinyl, cannot be changed as easily as wallpaper or paint. The sanitary appearance of a white surface is also a plus for many people. Fortunately, there are many ways to add depth and interest to a neutral palette. Neutral color schemes are not necessarily boring.

▶ The choice of a light beech wood for the cabinets keeps the mood of this space very open and airy.

DESIGN AND PHOTOGRAPHY COURTESY OF POGGENPOHL U. S. INC.

◀ White is the starting point in neutral interiors many home-owners favor. White denotes cleanliness and sanitary conditions, obviously an important consideration in the kitchen. However, this space is enriched with bold architectural details and a delicate fabric pattern, which adds interest and character to the generally monochromatic palette.

DESIGNER: MARILYN H. ROSE

▶ Traditional wood cabinets with a dark furniture-grade finish under granite counters send a message of quality to all who enter this impressive space. The medium-tan marble floors are a balance in color intensity. For many years this combination was the penultimate level of kitchen elegance. It still sets a standard of warmth and comfort.

DESIGNER: LILA LEVINSON

◄ White is sleek in this contemporary space, combining two eating areas in a glow of filtered and reflected light. The earth-tone tan ceramic floor is a good choice for practical clean-ability and also warms the cool white surfaces.

DESIGN AND PHOTOGRAPHY: COURTESY OF CHRISTOPHER PEACOCK KITCHENS, INC.

▶ The monotony of a white kitchen can be broken with a bold guest color, such as the shining green enamel stove, which is the hub of this carefully detailed space. The earth-tone ceramic floor is a natural platform for the stove and radiates warm color.

DESIGNER: JEANNE LEONARD

There are many subtle neutrals in this space, all honest to the materials and functions. A honey-colored floor, fresh white-painted cabinets, granite countertops, and ceramic backsplash surfaces each introduce a different color and texture. Palettes of neutral materials can be skillfully orchestrated for dramatic effects.

DESIGNER: DeGUILIO KITCHEN DESIGN, INC.

*Neutral colors can be
varied for subtle contrast
and depth.*

A black-and-white scheme is perhaps one step up the ladder of complexity from an all-white plan, but the contrast takes drama to an entirely different level of intensity. Many unusual details distinguish this space, beginning with the stainless graphic highlights that are strategically placed on vertical surfaces around the room, and the white stone counter with naturally chiseled edges.

Designer: Ed Winger

▲ The subtle hue of steel-gray cabinet fronts and the bright stainless highlights reveal that a skilled colorist planned this space.

DESIGNER: RAND ELLIOTT, FAIA

▲ There are many delightful surprises in this kitchen. The most obvious is the back-lit stained glass art, but many others hide around corners, such as the antiqued pine cabinet and the pierced-and-painted chairs. The combination of modern and traditional elements is eclectic; the stark modern cabinets serve as a blank canvas for more interesting details.

DESIGNER: DESIGN LOGIC LTD., INC.

▲ Rooster and hens with beams on the ceiling are classic early American, a comfort-
ng theme that includes many basic colors around the color wheel.

DESIGNER: TERI SEIDMAN

◀ Dominated by the black counters and white cabinets, primary "guest colors" are added in the stained glass ceiling lamp and red seat cushions.

DESIGNER: MONTE BERKOFF

◀ Black-and-white geometric wallpaper, black seats against white counters, and black hanging lamps against white walls make a contemporary drama achieved with careful editing of each element. Note that every item in the kitchen is carefully selected for its intrinsic color contribution.

The cocoa tile floor and countertops sandwich the creme-white cabinet faces, with just the stainless steel appliances bridging the gap. This is another very severely edited color plan that will reward a disciplined chef with a dramatic contemporary statement.
Designer: Robert Maddy

▲ This black-and-white color plan is not just "black and white."
Subtle shades of white, tan, and gray mediate the contrast.

DESIGN AND PHOTOGRAPHY COURTESY OF CHRISTOPHER PEACOCK KITCHENS, INC.

◀ The pale shades of white and tan, the rooster on the floor, and a sophisticated black granite counter are perhaps inspired by the colors of Tuscany. Note how the deeply set cabinet panels add strong shadow lines which become part of the overall color plan.

DESIGNER: ANNE COOPER

The materials and utensils of a kitchen provide limitless opportunities for variety of color and texture.

Warm natural wood finish of fine furniture quality softens the black-and-white ceramic backsplash and black counters. The choice of each material is a step in creating the color plan: a dab of white tile, a bold stroke of black granite, a wide wash of natural wood tone.

DESIGNER: DEGUILIO KITCHEN DESIGN, INC.

▲ The soft-gray cabinets and pastel colors in this space are very delicate, almost indistinguishable from white. The choice of a very light beech wood for the cabinets is an appropriately delicate touch that keeps the mood of this space very open and airy.

DESIGN AND PHOTOGRAPHY COURTESY OF POGGENPOHL U. S. INC.

▲ However traditional in style, this casual and light environment is absolutely up-to-date.
The hand-finished wood cabinets are light and unpretentious and the color plan is refreshing.
Note the white highlights in the wood grain and the floral hand decoration in a provincial
country style. Color is more than a superficial consideration.

DESIGNER: DAVID BARRETT

▲ There is warmth, interest, character, and the possibility of lasting pleasure for the fortunate person who will sip tea in this window seat. These are especially comfortable neutral colors, created through carefully mixed hue and intensity.

DESIGNER: SHELLEY AZAPIAN

▶ A very unusual combination of warm earthtones and contemporary geometry in black and white distinguishes this invigorating space. The floor and cabinets are almost the same hue and intensity, contrasting with the white ceramic counters and the vivid geometry of the counter edges and wallpaper. This space is comforting, but alive with delightful surprise.

DESIGNER: GAIL SHIELDS-MILLER

▲ Pierced-tin hutches flanking a bold stone fireplace are among the many elements that take this natural neutral color plan far outside the ordinary. The play of textures in the raw natural material is a part of the design artistry displayed here. It is a dramatic and comforting space.

DESIGNER: MARTIN KUCKLY

Another orchestration of several contrasting materials that lend natural color and a variety of slick metals beside toothy textures. The industrial-strength stove is a highlight that is found more frequently as homeowners cook less often but with more intensity.

DESIGNER: DAVID BARRETT

▲ This kitchen is whimsical and techy, with its elevated TV, neon art, and wall of windows.

DESIGNER: VINCE LATTUCA

Color and texture can create a very modern and high tech personality.

▲ A close-up reveals the subtle details of finish, glaze, and polished stone that are selected to create a deceptively simple design solution.

DESIGN AND PHOTOGRAPHY COURTESY OF CHRISTOPHER PEACOCK KITCHENS, INC.

◀ The wallpaper color echoes the edge trim on the cabinet doors. An interesting collection of memorabilia carries a crazy-quilt pattern into the eating area. This is a very comforting use of color and texture.

DESIGNER: DAVID BARRETT

▶ A glass-front refrigerator adds dimension to a white kitchen. White-textured backsplash tiles contrast nicely with the light mauve countertop.

DESIGNER: NANCY MULLAN

Flashing stainless steel surfaces surround a harlequin inlaid
design, a brilliant contrast certain to lift every moment.
This dramatic use of materials will inspire creativity.

DESIGNER: GAIL GREEN

◄ Mocha brown is an interesting and appetizing color for the cabinets, neutral but imaginative. A glorious bouquet of flowers glazed on the tile backsplash is an inspiring all-season focal point for the busy chef.

DESIGNER: ANNE COOPER

A greenhouse as a kitchen or kitchen as a greenhouse? This solarium provides the unique opportunity to grow herbs and flowers for their color, aroma, and beauty. The ceramic floor is a natural color and absorbs heat, but the stainless surfaces and the big black stove make this work-space really function. The neutral palette allows nature to have center stage.

DESIGNER: FOUR SEASONS GREENHOUSE

Put the spotlight on nature.

▼ Red-clay hexagonal tiles, light birch cabinetry, decorated ceramic tiles, and textured glass windows enliven this small space. The variety of materials and surface textures adds a special tactile quality to the confined work area.

DESIGNER: GAIL SHIELDS-MILLER

▲ Cast stone and metal against mottled cream walls bring nature inside. Note the twig curtain rod that carries the natural theme, color, and texture. A grass green rug and natural wood finish are part of the plan. The garden is coming inside.

DESIGNER: LILA LEVINSON

◀ Rough knotted-pine cabinets and barn beams are brightened with streams of natural light from skylights. Walls above the cabinets are brightened with a very light yellow hue. This space will glow with natural beauty.

DESIGNER: RAND ELLIOTT

The natural beauty of light playing upon warm wood casts a glow over the entire space.

FRIENDLY SCHEMES

For many people the kitchen is the heart of the home, a welcome place where information is exchanged among family members and where friends are introduced. In a busy household it is often the only place where everyone regularly sees each other. So, as the function becomes more important the choice of color for the setting might also be reconsidered.

Creating a mood that makes people feel welcome is a matter of choosing intensities and hues that are inviting. The use of color on kitchen cabinets, floors, and ceilings is very common. Warm tints of blue and green are especially popular. Patterns that are present can be inviting and reassuring. Materials that have a texture or grain such as cool, dark cobblestone or a muddy, warm wood surface pique one's sensory experience, providing a place where people can be open, and interaction is inevitable.

▶ Dark-green kitchen cabinets almost always establish a country mood, here enlivened by the natural light from the French doors and windows.

Designer: N.J. Monthly Magazine

◀ Creamy yellow cabinets and movie studio-type lighting above bring a spell of quiet surprise to the sculptural floor plan. The yellow is a good mood lifter for this confined area.

DESIGNER: GAIL SHIELDS-MILLER

◀ Soft blue-and-white checked walls frame a stained-glass window with very rich cream-colored cabinets and many fine details. The cook will enjoy working in this pantry.

DESIGNER: D'IMAGE

▲ A lovely shade of blue defined with trellis-type trim and an arch
in the ceiling create an exciting arbor in this most unusual treatment
of space. It is easy to imagine dinner guests wanting to be in the
kitchen while the meal is still on the stove.

DESIGNER: STEPHAN AND GAIL HUBERMAN

A friendly place.

◀ Deep dusty-green walls are an understated background with a look of mellow age in this country theme. The green hue was carefully chosen to achieve exactly the right effect.

DESIGNER: RONALD BRICKE

▶ Blue is a very popular color in kitchens, and it can be varied with many levels of intensity. The breadboard creates interesting shadow lines, as do the paneled doors. White handles and trim give crisp definition to the fields of blue color.

DESIGN AND PHOTOGRAPHY COURTESY OF
CHRISTOPHER PEACOCK KITCHENS, INC.

▲ This all-white kitchen is accented with a blue backsplash. The white cathedral ceiling over the white cabinetry creates an unusual sense of floating within this airy space.

DESIGNER: TOM F. LECKSTROM

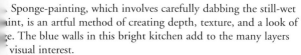

◀ Sponge-painting, which involves carefully dabbing the still-wet paint, is an artful method of creating depth, texture, and a look of age. The blue walls in this bright kitchen add to the many layers of visual interest.

DESIGNER: NANCY MULLAN

▲ This very unusual shade of navy blue, framed in black, infuses the space with warmth and a certain international sophistication. The bright lipstick red in the painting and the roses is a carefully orchestrated guest color, a clue to professional planning.

DESIGN AND PHOTOGRAPHY COURTESY OF POGGENPOHL U.S. INC.

Spaces that invite family and friends to linger.

◄ This is a dark workspace that wraps rich color, texture, and detail around all sides. It is very warm and comforting, a mood preferred by many who see their home as a refuge.

DESIGNER: PATRICIA KOCAK

◀ Another use of creamy yellow, contrasting with black and hard shadow lines. The use of color contrast and lighting creates drama, but this palette requires skilled manipulation.

DESIGNER: GAIL SHIELDS-MILLER

Dark-green kitchen cabinets almost always establish a country mood,
here enlivened by the natural light from the French doors and windows.
Adequate light, always needed for work surfaces, must be carefully planned
when wide areas of dark color are used.

Designer: N.J. Monthly Magazine

▶ Above the tile backsplash is a sky-blue wall that inspires the mood of this space for a talented bread baker and gourmet chef. Color high on a wall and on the ceiling can transform the mood of a room.

DESIGNER: LILA LEVINSON

Colorful details make the difference.

Pink is the lightest tint of red, and it is an imaginative choice for the kitchen.
Clearly it works very well with the rich speckled tint of the Corian counters and
the brass hardware.

DESIGNER: NANCY MULLAN

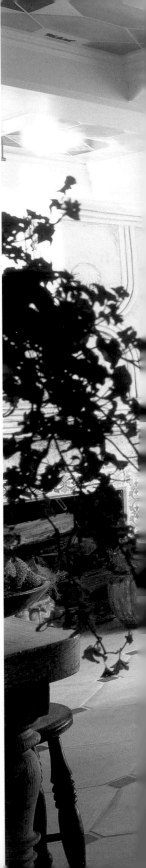

*Feature
a colorful
collection of
culinary tools.*

This is one of the most extraordinary kitchen design projects ever photographed, and a benchmark for imaginative use of color as well as rare natural materials. Although out-of-reach of many budgets, it is a project that stirs the imagination and may lead to some affordable design ideas. The ceiling treatment in tile reminds one that ceilings are a place for color and pattern. The sponge-painted walls can easily be emulated by an ambitious amateur. Yellow and green is a sure-to-please palette foundation, partly because it is the combination of color one sees in spring leaves.

DESIGNER: BARBARA OSTROM

▶ This view shows the lovely table, wrought iron chandelier, and tiled ceiling.

DESIGNER: BARBARA OSTROM

The cooking alcove has a tiled wall and hanging copper pots.

Designer: Barbara Ostrom

Well-used copper and brass adds character and autheticity.

COLORS FOR INTIMATE INDIVIDUALITY

The frequency with which people entertain in the home varies greatly. Some people entertain for business purposes, some have large extended families, and many simply enjoy having friends in their home. Those who entertain frequently usually put a higher priority on decorating and furnishings. Guests wander into the kitchen to watch the hors d'oeuvres being prepared or perhaps to participate in creating a culinary masterpiece. Food preparation is theater and the kitchen is now a stage.

The color palettes are now far afield from the plain generic-white variety. Complex color plans, elegant surface decoration, and rare materials enliven this active space. These plans are more intimate because they reveal more personality. Palettes in these kitchens may be confined to a very small group of colors to enhance intimacy and unite the space. Accents tend to draw the eye and bring whimsy and unique appeal to the room.

▶ Contemporary whimsy mixes red and black. Large areas of white will mediate the contrasts.

DESIGNER: VOGEL-MULLA

imaginative and rich tint of yellow with surprise bursts of red and blue, there is great artistry in this palette
nd in the textures. The beaded board adds good shadow lines and all of the cabinetry is out of the ordinary.
Wide pine floorboards are difficult to find, but the warmth of the finished color is worth the trouble. These
oors and all of the surfaces will age to a mellow patina. Fine natural materials improve with time.

ESIGNER: D'IMAGE

► A retro early American mood is comforting with red-brick and blue-patterned fabric and wallpaper.

DESIGNER: DAVID BARRETT

◀ A barrel-vaulted ceiling with a country scene painted at one end is the penultimate solution to boring ceilings. Although out-of-reach for many, this design inspires many thoughts about pattern-on-pattern and the value of using good materials. Every corner can be the subject for imaginative use of color, pattern, and texture.

DESIGNER: BARBARA OSTROM

▶ Very understated yet colorful, the low intensity tints of blue are anchored in the deeper blue of the floor tiles. Notice that the paneled doors of the cabinets have been highlighted with a pastel tint of the blue. Yellow is sparingly used as a second color. Blue and yellow together are often found in nautical themes, which leads one to wonder if this entire room was inspired by the blue of the sea reflecting a light blue sky.

DESIGNER: JEFFREY B. HAINES

◄ Green tone-on-tone wallpaper and a faux-marble paint surface on the cabinets seem to reflect an effort to achieve elegance, perhaps honoring the gilded ancestor? Humor is a valid mood, especially for this entertaining area.

DESIGNER: BARBARA OSTROM

◀ The combination of mauve-washed walls, white cabinets, and wood barchairs transform the kitchen area into a space that encourages comraderie and the enjoyment of a satisfying meal.

DESIGNER: JEFFREY B. HAINES

Add warmth with carefully selected tints of red.

▶ Plum is an excellent tint of red in the kitchen because it adds excitement without jarring the senses, and it is an attractive hue. Notice how the black counters are echoed in the dark chocolate floor and dark ceiling trim.

Plum-red walls extend into the dining area, bathed in light from the window alcove.

DESIGNER: LEONARDIS KITCHEN INTERIORS

he primary colors add personality
ıd lift the mood of the kitchen.

▶ The tantalizing colors of milk chocolate brown with sunshine yellow, and the light from the solarium ceiling will certainly make this narrow space alive.

DESIGNER: PROFESSIONAL BUILDER MAGAZINE

▲ This is a carefully planned retro color scheme, echoing the first formica and chrome kitchens of the 50s.

DESIGNER: AL EVANS

▶ View from kitchen to wine tasting table, note ceiling detail which could be emulated.

◀ This is an ideal setting for wine tasting, a virtual and actual bouquet of color to tantalize the senses. Note the stenciled ribbon motif at the window, the type of detail that distinguishes elegant design. There are books and magazine articles that show the amateur how to create these effects, and lately many professional painters have been trained in stenciling and hand-decorating.

DESIGNER: BARBARA OSTROM

▶ Computers are becoming the nerve center of many homes, and plans should include a place as attractive as this in or near the kitchen. Notice the mottled walls in gray and the lavish use of pattern in the tiles and wallpaper. Every surface has been given careful and individual design attention.

DESIGNER: BARBARA OSTROM

▲ The tint of the yellow cabinets is carefully modulated to ...ow with warmth. Two patterns live happily with one ...nother, the tile backsplash and the wallpaper.

...ESIGNER: BARBARA EBERLEIN

▲ Light blue and pink is an imaginative combination in the kitchen, and creates a very personal space. A settee on one side of the table instead of a chair demonstrates uninhibited personal style.

DESIGNER: LEE'S INTERIOR DESIGN SERVICES, INC.

◀ Blood-red walls, white
and warm wood cabinets,
and a green floral area rug
make a lively formula for
stimulating color. Notice
that the wood finish and
white-painted cabinets
complement each other.
The concept of designing
everything in the kitchen
to match is not necessary.
One can choose uniformity,
which is very reassuring, or
elect to mix colors, textures,
and materials for more
variety.

DESIGNER: MONTE BERKOFF

Victorian pink and blue with light and bright detail all
around invites civility within this special corner of the world.

DESIGNER: SUSIE LEADER

A white kitchen surrounded with lavender and spice-color red tiles and fabrics is invigorating. The wide areas of white frame the bright highlights, focusing attention on the color.

▲ Black kitchen cabinets, with a red accent wall facing black
Roman shades, is perhaps the extreme of dramatic black kitchens.
Black connotes sophistication, especially in a metropolitan environment. It can be serene, and it draws from many international design
concepts.

DESIGNER: VOGEL-MULEA

Contemporary whimsy mixes red, black, and white with streams of natural light. Large areas of white will mediate the contrasts and soften the intensity of color in this space.

DESIGNER: VOGEL-MULEA

THE REJUVENATING BATHROOM

▲ The potential for a very personal area that will be used every day pushes the design challenge. This might be a very ordinary bathroom except for the furniture and accessories which replay and enliven the palette. As ceramic tiles and porcelain fixtures are difficult and expensive to replace, this is a good tactic for improving space quickly and easily.

DESIGNER: LILA LEVINSON

The bathroom qualifies as a sanctuary. Relaxing in a tub full of warm water topped with soothing mounds of fragrant bubbles is the way many people wash away their daily stresses and renew themselves. Many new homes have master bathrooms with whirlpools and saunas, connected to the bedroom suite in such a way that the entire bedroom and bath are one area devoted to personal restoration. This presents a design challenge as potentially fulfilling as any in the home, and one that must include a wide range of conditions and materials.

Consider ten of the most important requirements:

1. Sanitary
2. Private
3. Quiet
4. Fresh
5. Permanent
6. Comfortable
7. Safe
8. Personal
9. Restful
10. Rejuvenating

Meeting all of these criteria requires a complete review of options, including color. The restful mood, the regenerative atmosphere, the safe lighting levels, and the fresh appearance will all depend on a well-chosen color palette.

The following examples of fine bathroom design are arranged in the order of color palette, from neutral through analogous to complementary.

▶ The pinks in this marble reflect attractive color. An out-of-this-world barreled ceiling with trompe l'oeil clouds puts the virtual lid on this extraordinary space.

DESIGNER: BARBARA EBERLEIN

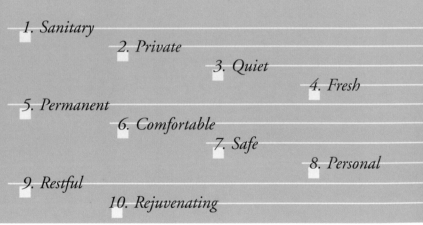

PALETTES FOR PRIVACY AND SIMPLICITY

Most bathrooms are very simple. Contractors often select white fixtures and tiles because this will offend the fewest prospective buyers, although it might not delight anyone. But the following bathrooms are carefully balanced and demonstrate how textures, earth tones, and small spots of color can delight the eye.

Palettes in private, simple spaces may be confined to one, two or three hues, integrating neutrals with splashes of color. Smooth, monochromatic surfaces soothe the eye, and simple natural patterns calm the soul.

▶ Earth-tone browns and lighter beige on textur[e] ceramic tiles are very warm and reassuring.

A consistent pattern of blue on white is a fresh color scheme that adds dimension to this thoughtfully planned bathroom. The many storage areas, which are the functional foundation of this area, become striking in pattern and dimension. The floor is earth-tone brown and tan, a natural color solution that adds warmth to the cool white and blue.

DESIGNER: DEGUILIO KITCHEN DESIGN, INC.

▲ White marble with broad veins of gray and the gray
metal sculpture with black-and-white art photography tie
this contemporary plan together into a cohesive signature.

DESIGNER: FLOYD ANDERSON

Contrasting panels of rich color.

◀ Red is the guest color in this color plan, invigorating an otherwise calm overall tan palette. The toy soldiers add a whimsical touch.

DESIGNER: AL EVANS

◄ The sponge-painted walls add depth to the medium green, a tint of the porcelain tile color. Drapery fringe and towels pick up the green theme, which is very refreshing against large areas of white tile.

DESIGNER: SUSAN VANDENHEUVEL

Color, smooth as silk.

◀ Trompe l'oeil twig design on cabinets and wall carries a natural neutral palette around the room. Hand decoration on walls is a traditional art form that flourished in Europe during the eighteenth century. Although relatively expensive, this technique is especially delightful in a small, intimate space.

DESIGNER: DAVID BARRETT

Delightful hand decoration.

Earth-tone browns and lighter beige on textured ceramic tiles are very warm and reassuring, wrapping the room in comfortable colors. Large sources of light lift the spirit but require convenient controls for privacy.

FRESH AND COMFORTABLE COLOR SCHEMES

Adding stronger color to the bathroom may bring it into the flow of nearby rooms. The choices are wide, and because the room is small the color palette will have impact. Green, blue, and yellow are often selected because they are comfortable colors and imply natural freshness. The bath can be theatrical too, with imaginative decorative treatments.

Citrus colors and fruity hues may lend a healthy feel to a small space, while bold, individualized accents add personal value and comfort. An eclectic scheme may bring out the best in a room, and well-being from within.

▶ The ceiling swags carry the eye down and across more interesting color.

A gleaming hunter-green counter is fresh and easy to keep
clean. Note the subtle paint technique on the cabinets, which
involves using a deeper tint to frame the architectural elements.

DESIGNER: BARBARA EBERLEIN

◄ A masculine mood is created by the use of deep-brown wood tones, brass hardware, and the solid black-gray marble surfaces. There is a very light faux-marble pattern on the walls, which balances the transition between the deeper hues.

DESIGNER: BARBARA EBERLEIN

◀ This is a fantasyland of color, pattern, and theme, which will lift the mood of every fortunate guest for many years. Garden and trellis painting on walls is a very old technique in decoration and is most appropriate in small spaces.

DESIGNER: BONNIE SIRACUSA, MURALIST

A floral-skirted vanity that echoes the painted faux window and faux view of a lake is bathed in the healthy glow of a medium-pink tint. The delight of this two-room bath suite will make the effort worthwhile.

DESIGNER: OLD WORLD INTERIORS

◀ Faux bamboo door and walls with delicately painted blue, gold, and white porcelain fixtures distinguish this lavishly designed space.

DESIGNER: DAVID BARRETT

Fantasyland revisited with a desert tent, doubled by a large mirror. Although very complex and busy, the effect is under control because the colors are almost all neutrals, except high on the walls and on the ceiling.

DESIGNER: DAVID BARRETT

◄ This would be a very stuffy space were it not for the clever use of brass accents and the unusual crisp blue paint and wallpaper hue.

DESIGNER: FRIDERIKE KEMP AND JEAN SIMMERS

A private space rich with personal interest.

◀ Obviously, bathrooms have great potential. This rich green space dispels many preconceptions of the boring bath.

DESIGNER: CAROLYN BRONSON

▲ Fantasy with fabric: the ceiling is tented and swags carry the sift theme down and across more interesting color.

▲ Some rooms have the elusive characteristic that can only be described as "wow." This topiary theme introduces green tints, a comfortable color.

DESIGNER: DAVID BARRETT

◄ Purple, pink, blue, and green all live happily together in this lively space where fabric and wall covering have been used to great effect. This is a complex palette.

HUES FOR REJUVENATION

Technology has increased the pace of our lives. Instant e-mail, overnight express mail, one-day worldwide jet travel all spin us faster than we ever imagined. By evening we need a full restoration of all of our systems, a top-to-bottom overhaul of our senses. The design of the modern bathroom serves this.

Every room in the home reveals someone's personality. It may reveal shyness, or a more outgoing character. The bathroom can be like a piece of custom jewelry, designed with one special personality in mind. Because the room is small, it lends itself to more rarefied treatments that would be overwhelming or prohibitively expensive in other rooms.

▶ This small room is like stepping into a modern painting.

DESIGNER: JOY LICHT

Red is very often a misunderstood color. In the hands of a skilled colorist it can be warm and comforting. Note how the large areas of red are broken with a light pattern.

DESIGNER: JOSEF PRICCI

◀ Lavender floral
wallpaper and the
pastel flame-stitch
shower curtain bathe
this room in warmth.

◀ High-tech, neon-blue mirrors and a rich navy blue tile introduce a fresh nautical mood, due to the large contrasting areas of pure white. The scheme is as crisp as a sailor's uniform.

DESIGNER: ULTIMATE SOUND INSTALLATIONS, INC.

. Almost all gray, the pinpoint spots of electric
ue create excitement and drama.

SIGNER: VOGEL-MULEA

Serene color.

It is easy to see that a room is like a painting, and the palette can include many different materials. There is an enormous selection of color in fixtures, tiles and accessories. This small room is like stepping into a modern painting.

DESIGNER: JOY LICHT

◄ Rose damask wallpaper carries a pink cast into this inviting space. Note the scalloped white sinks and marble tile floor.

DESIGNER: BARBARA EBERLEIN

◀ A coordinated trellis pattern on the walls, tiles, and down into the sink bowl has impact and carries the natural green in various intensities. This type of garden theme is always welcome in a bath, especially the guest bathroom.

DESIGNER: COUNTRY FLOORS

▶ Small accents of contrasting green and red enliven this otherwise plain room. The accessories have been selected to elaborate the color theme.

DESIGNER: LILA LEVINSON

Every available surface has been treated with enriching color variation to create a total look of understated elegance. Texture is used throughout this room. Note that the larger tiles have been bordered by small mosaic tiles, a technique that is within the skill range of many craftsmen.

DESIGNER: FRED KENTOP AND LINDA MALKIN

◀ Tone-on-tone green striped wallpaper with marble and rich wood tones set a mood of elegance and regenerating serenity. The artwork over the whirlpool island is a good visual method of centering the space.

DESIGNER: STEPHEN AND GAIL HUBERMAN

◀ Various tints of red, from rose to pink warm this room. Gray and pink is a combination that was very popular in the 1950s, and has come back because it is very attractive.

DESIGNER: ANN HEFFERNAN

Pink is a warm, restful choice in the bath. The floor is a
nt of the wall color.

ESIGNER: LISE LAWSON

There is a botanical theme to this delicate space,
which has decided the entire color palette. There
is a perfect palette in every garden.

DESIGNER: LISE LAWSON

Nature is always welcome.

Teal is a time-honored tint of green which has a special quality that
sets the mood. This is a simple, crisp, and fresh plan that will endure
for years. Color plans that involve ceramic tile installations cannot be
changed easily, a reason to avoid color trends that have short life spans.

DESIGNER: PROFESSIONAL BUILDER MAGAZINE.

▲ The natural figure of the fine wood veneers on the cabinets has been colored to match the natural gray-green marble accents. Wood color is part of the palette. Many imaginative color themes are possible with wood stains.

DESIGNER: CATHI MANKOWSKI

◄ Lavender ribbons painted on the floor and bouquets of color high on the wall under a green ceiling are just a few of the details which build toward the ultimate success of this plan for a small room. Trellis woodwork and a pedestal sink with flowers complete the picture.

DESIGNER: JULIE BOYNTON

▲ Detail of skirted table.

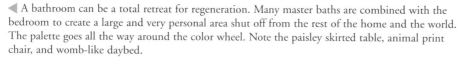 A bathroom can be a total retreat for regeneration. Many master baths are combined with the bedroom to create a large and very personal area shut off from the rest of the home and the world. The palette goes all the way around the color wheel. Note the paisley skirted table, animal print chair, and womb-like daybed.

DESIGNER: J. ALLEN MURPHY & ASSOCIATES

▲ Detail of daybed with slipper storage and soldier wallpaper.

▲ Sink and paisley cafe curtains.

A luxurious Victorian theme and mood are established with the romantic lavender hue in this delicate bathroom suite. The complex authentic trim and openwork are featured with gleaming white that contrasts against the soft lavender wall pattern. Brass fixtures shine like jewelry and every color detail has been carefully planned to increase the effect of this regenerating space.

DESIGNER: ANNE COOPER

DRAMATIC COLOR

The bathroom can be a very dramatic space, because the surfaces are all very close, and there is a sense of enclosure. Like a Fabergé egg, elegant small detail will delight the senses. This is often the intent in guest bathrooms.

Intense color is awe-inspiring; deep unified palettes move us to react to our surroundings and experience the space in a radical way.

▶ Bright, hot contrast of black and white and red will surprise the visitor to this room. A mirrored ceiling lifts the drama one notch higher.

DESIGNER: MICHAEL deSANTIS

◀ The red striped wallpaper with contrasting textures and polished brass fixtures over a gold sink are crowned by the dramatic gilded mirror. The black marble counter is a solid anchor.

DESIGNER: PENNE POOLE

◀ Bright yellow walls adorned with a painted floral swag are the dramatic features, further highlighted with a scalloped sink and gold and brass accents.

DESIGNER: NORMAN MICHAELOFF

◀ Bright, hot contrast of black and white and red will surprise the visitor to this room. The fixtures and frames are like geometric graphics against the dark background. A mirrored ceiling lifts the drama one notch higher.

DESIGNER: MICHAEL deSANTIS

. Black, blue, and another very cosmopolitan contemporary
heme. The geometry of this plan is echoed in many details.

SIGNER: MARY KNACHSTEDT

◀ Black and silver wall covering with chrome hardware and highlights are the formula in this bath. The most dramatic plans often involve just two very strong dark colors; black is frequently used, especially in guest bathrooms.

DESIGNER: DAVID BARRETT

Another kind of drama is exhibited by the unusual color tints of this
Southwestern theme: peach, gray, clay, and a blue sky over the log beams.
DESIGNER: PROFESSIONAL BUILDER MAGAZINE

...ed of just the right tint is at the same time ...oth classic and dramatic. Note the two ...osaics of distinguished portraits on the wall ...ove the tub.

SIGNER: DENNIS ROLLAND

Through the shower one can see the bright yellow hand-painted fabric panel, which is a guest color in this carefully planned color scheme.

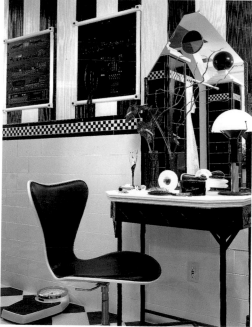

The soccer balls in the bathtub mimic the stark black-and-white theme that has been developed with ceramic tiles in this remarkable room.

DESIGNER: IVAN DOLAN AND DEBBIE HABICHT

A vanity table and audio equipment maintain the theme.

▶ This might have been an ordinary little bathroom if a talented designer had not added the bright fabrics, a richly patterned screen, and yellow walls.

DESIGNER: SAMUEL BOTERO ASSOCIATES, INC.

◀ Rich traditional elegance with fine cherry
wood solids and veneers, veined marble counters,
and authentic gilded mirror frames are another
more reserved approach to drama.

DESIGNER: DAVID BARRETT

DIRECTORY OF INTERIOR DESIGNERS

Floyd Anderson
Lohan Associates
225 N. Michigan Ave.
Chicago, IL 60601
ph. 312/938-4455
fax 312/938-0929
100

Audio Design Associates
602 Mamaroneck Ave.
White Plains, NY 10605
ph. 914/946-9595
fax 914/946-9620
16

Shelley Azapian
Address not available
42

David Barrett, FASID
131 East 71st St.
New York, NY 10021
ph. 212/585-3180
fax 212/585-3246
41, 45, 47, 76, 104, 112, 113, 116, 146, 153

Monte Berkoff, CKD
Herbert P. Bisulk, Inc.
295 Nassau Blvd.
Garden City South, NY 11530
ph. 516/483-0377
fax 516/565-4191
32, 89

Samuel Botero Associates, Inc.
420 E. 54th St., Suite 34-G
New York, NY 10022
ph. 212/935-5155
fax 212/832-0714
152

Julie Boynton
JCB Interiors
1689 The Great Road
Skillman, NJ 08558
ph. 609/466-2569
135

Ronald Bricke, honorary member ASID
Ronald Bricke & Assocs.
333 E. 69th St.
New York, NY 10021
ph. 212/472-9006
fax 212/472-9008
59

Carolyn Bronson
Address not available
115

John Buscarello, ASID
27 West 20th Street
Suite 1206
New York, NY 10011
ph. 212/691-5881
cover

Anne Cooper, allied member ASID
Anne Cooper Interiors, Inc.
80 Clark Rd.
Bernardsville, NJ 07924
ph. 908/696-0464
fax 908/696-0490
37, 49, 138, 139

Country Floors
15 E. 16th St.
New York, NY 10003
ph. 212/627-8300
7, 126

Crossville Mosaics
P.O. Box 1168
Crossville, TN 38557
ph. 931/484-2110
cover

deGuilio kitchen design, inc.
1121 Central Ave.
Wilmette, IL 60091
ph. 847/256-8833
fax 847/256-8842
20, 26, 27, 38, 39, 98, 99

Michael deSantis, ASID
Michael deSantis, Inc.
1110 Second Ave.
New York, NY 10022
ph. 212/753-8871
5, 141, 144

Design Logic Ltd., Inc.
409 Little Silver Rt. Rd.
Little Silver, NJ 07739
30

D'Image
Address not available
57, 74, 75

Ivan Dolan and Debbie Habicht
P.O. Box 1299
Bayshore, NJ 11706
ph. 516/666-1868
50, 151

Barbara Eberlein, ASID
Eberlein Design Consultants Ltd.
809 Walnut St., Suite 401
Philadelph.ia, PA 19103
ph. 215/405-0400
fax 215/405-0588
13, 17, 87, 95, 108, 125

Rand Elliott, FAIA
Elliott & Associates Architects
35 Harrison Ave.
Oklahome City, OK 73104
ph. 405/232-9554
fax 405/232-9997
10, 30, 53

Euro-Concepts Ltd.
1802 E. Jericho Tpke.
Huntington, NY 11743
14

Al Evans
Address not available
83, 102

Four Seasons Greenhouses
Address not available
50, 51

Michael R. Golden Design
37 West 20th Street
New York, NY 10011
ph. 212/645-3001
fax 212/645-3003
cover

Gail Green
Green & Company, Inc.
Interior Designers
110 East 50th St.
New York, NY 10022
48

Jeffrey B. Haines, ASID
Butler's of Far Hills
53 Route 202 South
Far Hills, NJ 07931
ph. 908/234-1764
78, 80

Ann Heffernan
Address not available
15, 130

Stephen and Gail Huberman
SGH Designs, Inc.
P.O. Box 535
Pound Ridge, NY 10576
ph. 914/764-8042
58, 129

Fred Kentop and Linda Malkin
K Design
938 Port Washington Blvd.
Port Washington, NY 11050
128

Friderike Kemp and Jean Simmers
Jean P. Simmers, Ltd.
24 Smith St.
Rye, NY 10580
ph. 914/967-8533
fax 914/967-6085
114

Mary Knackstedt, ASID
Knackstedt, Inc.
2901 N. Front St.
Harrisburg, PA 17110
ph. 717/233-6575
145

Patricia Kocak
Patricia Kocak Interiors
202 Lexow Ave.
Upper Nyack, NY 10960
ph. 914/358-8805
fax 914/358-8805
9, 63

Martin Kuckly
Kuckly Associates, Inc.
506 East 74th Street, #5J
New York, NY 10011
44

Vince Lattuca
Visconti & Co., Inc.
245 E. 57th St.
New York, NY 10022
ph. 212/758-2720
fax 212/758-2731
46

Lise Lawson
Lise Lawson ID, Ltd.
6420 North Lake Dr.
Fox Point, WI 53217
ph. 414/351-6334
131, 132

Susie Leader
Susie Leader Interiors
1280 Latham
Birmingham, MI 48009
ph. 248/642-2571
fax 248/642-9897
62, 90

Tom F. Leckstrom, CKD
Kitchen and Bath Designs Unlimited
5 Parker Rd.
Osterville, MA 02655
ph. 508/428-3999
fax 508/420-3640
61

Lee's Interior Design Services, Inc.
55 Woodland Dr.
Oyster Bay Cove, NY 11771
ph. 516/922-5647
88, 101

Jeanne Leonard
Jeanne Leonard Interiors
10 Beach Rd.
Westhampton Beach, NY 11978
25

Leonardis Kitchen Interiors
35 Airport Rd., Ste. LL20
Morristown, NJ 07960
ph. 973/829-7112
fax 973/829-7116
81

Lila Levinson, ASID, CKD, CID
Accent on Design
2075 De La Cruse Blvd., #101
Santa Clara, CA 95050
ph. 408/988-4600
24, 52, 66, 127

Joy Licht
Cayley Barrett Assoc., Ltd.
238 East Grand St.
Fleetwood, NY 10552
ph. 914/667-4527
fax 914/667-4658
119, 124

Robert Maddy, AIA
1175 Montauk Hwy.
West Islip, NY 11795
ph. 516/587-4199
fax 516/587-5030
35

Cathi Mankowski
CDM Designs, Inc.
20 Reservoir Rd.
Melville, NY 11747
ph. 516/549-0050
fax 516/549-0048
18, 134

Norman Michaeloff
Norman Michaeloff Interior Design, Inc.
177 East 75th St.
New York, NY 10021
ph. 212/288-5400
fax 212/288-5400
143

Nancy Mullan, ASID, CKD
NDM Kitchens
204 E. 77th St.
New York, NY 10021
ph. 212/628-4629
fax 212/628-6738
47, 61, 67

J. Allen Murphy & Associates
Address not available
136, 137

N.J. Monthly Magazine
Address not available
55, 65

Nova Studios
Address not available
34

Old World Interiors
Address not available
111

Barbara Ostrom
Barbara Ostrom Assoc.
1 International Blvd., Suite 209
Mahwah, NJ 07495
ph. 201/529-0444
3, 4, 12, 13, 19, 68, 69, 70, 71, 77, 79, 84, 85, 86

Christopher Peacock Kitchens, Inc.
151 Greenwich Ave.
Greenwich, CT 06830
ph. 203/862-9333
11, 25, 36, 43, 46, 60

Poggenpohl U.S. Inc.
145 US Hwy. 46 W   Suite 200
Wayne, NJ -7470
23, 40, 62

Penne Poole
Penne Poole Interior Design, Inc.
3410 Prospect St.
Georgetown
Washington, D.C 20007
142

Josef Pricci
737 Park Ave.
New York, NY 10021
ph. 212/570-2140
20

Professional Builder Magazine
350 E. Touchy
Des Plaines, IL 60018
ph. 847/390-2105
fax 847/635-9950
2, 133, 147

Dennis Rolland
Dennis Rolland, Inc.
05 E. 54th St.
New York, NY 10022
ph. 212/644-0537
48, 149

Marilyn H. Rose
Marilyn H. Rose Interiors
4 Birch Hill Rd.
Locust Valley, NY 11560
24

Teri Seidman
150 East 61st St.
New York, NY 10021
ph. 212/888-6551
fax 212/888-8356
4, 31

Gail Shields-Miller
Shields & Company Interiors
149 Madison Ave., Suite 201
New York, NY 10016
ph. 212/679-9130
fax 212/679-9140
43, 52, 56, 64

Bonnie Siracusa
Bonnie Siracusa Art Studio
205 Jerome St.
Syosset, NY 11791
ph. 516/433-7050
110

Ultimate Sound Installations, Inc.
36-16 29th St.
Long Island City, NY 11106
ph. 718/729-2111
fax 718/729-2126
122

Susan VandenHeuvel
144 Main St.
Port Washington, NY 11771
103

Vogel-Mulea
Address not Available
73, 92, 93, 123

Winger, CKD
Thurston Kitchen & Bath
2920 E. 6th Ave.
Denver, CO 80206
ph. 303/399-4564
fax 303/399-3179
28, 29

DIRECTORY OF PHOTOGRAPHERS

Hedrich Blessing, Ltd.
Robert Shimer
Chris Barrett
John Miller
Bill Hedrich
11 W. Illinois
Chicago, IL 60610
ph. 312/321-1151
fax 312/321-1165
10, 26, 27, 30, 38, 39, 51, 82, 100, 101, 102, 133, 147

Bill Rothschild
19 Judith Lane
Wesley Hills, NY 10952
ph. 914/354-4567
4, 11, 14, 19, 24, 25, 31, 32, 34, 35, 37, 42, 43, 44, 45, 47, 49, 50, 62, 64, 76, 79, 84, 91, 98, 103, 105, 110, 112, 113, 117, 134, 143, 145, 146, 153

Phillip Ennis
Phillip Ennis Photography
114 Millertown Rd.
Bedford, NY 10506
ph. 914/354-4567 (evenings);
212/752-3674 (days)
5, 9, 12, 13, 15, 17, 30, 33, 46, 47, 48, 49, 52, 53, 57, 58, 60, 63, 65, 67, 68, 69, 70, 71, 74, 75, 77, 78, 80, 81, 85, 91, 92, 93, 99, 111, 114, 115, 116, 117, 120, 121, 122, 123, 124, 128, 130, 131, 135, 136, 137, 138, 139, 142, 144, 148, 149, 150, 151, 152

Tom Crane
Tom Crane Photography, Inc.
113 Cumberland Place
Bryn Mawr, PA 19010
ph. 610/525-2444
5, 12, 16, 88, 95, 109, 125

Susan English
234 Cook St. #2
Denver, CO 80206
28, 29

Michael Hill
333 E. 69th St.
New York, NY 10021
ph. 212/472-9006
fax 212/472-9008
59

Dan Forer
Forer, Inc.
6815 SW 81st Terrace
Miami, FL 33143
ph. 305/667-3646
fax 305/667-4733
83

Tim Lee Photography
2 Zachary Lane
New Milford, CT 06776
ph. 860/355-4661
fax: 860/350-3526
cover

ABOUT THE AUTHORS

John and Melanie Aves met in their art and English classes at Albion College in Michigan, a forecast of the three decades they have spent together exploring design, literature and education. Melanie has been associated with various schools and universities as teacher, professor, and a lifelong student in the field of art and journalism. John consults with several home furnishings companies on marketing and design development. They have been involved with the publication of over 20 books on interior design many of which have been translated into several languages and are sold throughout the world. The Aves have three daughters and live in a restored 110-year-old French Victorian style cottage overlooking Macatawa bay in western Michigan.